W9-AFS-753

Popular Cat Library

Birman Cat

Karen Commings

Published in association with T.F.H. Publications, Inc.,
the world's largest and most respected publisher of pet literature

Chelsea House Publishers
Philadelphia

CONTENTS

History of the Birman 3
Birman Character 8
The Birman Standard and Colors 14
Selecting a Birman 21
General Care and Grooming 31
Feeding Birmans 39
Health Care 46
Exhibiting Birmans 58
Index 64

Popular Cat Library

Abyssinian Cat
American Shorthair Cat
Bengal Cat
Birman Cat
Burmese Cat
Exotic Shorthair Cat
Himalayan Cat
Maine Coon Cat
Persian Cat
Ragdoll Cat
Scottish Fold Cat
Siamese Cat

This edition © TFH Publications, Inc., 1 TFH Plaza, Neptune City, NJ 07753. This special library bound edition is made expressly for Chelsea House Publishers, a division of Main Line Book Company.

Library of Congress Cataloging-in-Publication Data

Commings, Karen.
Guide to owning a Birman / by Karen Commings.
p.   cm. — (Popular cat library)
Summary: A guide to the history, feeding, grooming, exhibition, temperament, health, and breeding of Birman cats.
ISBN 0-7910-5460-8 (hc.)
1. Birman cat Juvenile literature.   [1. Birman cat. 2. Cats. 3. Pets.]
I. Title. II. Series.
SF449.B5C86 1999
636.8'3—dc21   99-36717
                                                            CIP

The Guide to
Owning a
Birman Cat

Karen Commings

CONTENTS

History of the Birman 3

Birman Character 8

The Birman Standard and Colors 14

Selecting a Birman 21

General Care and Grooming 31

Feeding Birmans 39

Health Care 46

Exhibiting Birmans 58

Index 64

Photo Credits: Gale Blonar, Karen Commings, Isabelle Francais, Gibraltar, Caroline Leibman, Jan Rogers, Debbie Sperry, Jane Stiner.

RE-411

© T.F.H. Publications, Inc.

Distributed in the UNITED STATES to the Pet Trade by T.F.H. Publications, Inc., 1 TFH Plaza, Neptune City, NJ 07753; on the Internet at www.tfh.com; in CANADA by Rolf C. Hagen Inc., 3225 Sartelon St., Montreal, Quebec H4R 1E8; Pet Trade by H & L Pet Supplies Inc., 27 Kingston Crescent, Kitchener, Ontario N2B 2T6; in ENGLAND by T.F.H. Publications, PO Box 74, Havant PO9 5TT; in AUSTRALIA AND THE SOUTH PACIFIC by T.F.H. (Australia), Pty. Ltd., Box 149, Brookvale 2100 N.S.W., Australia; in NEW ZEALAND by Brooklands Aquarium Ltd., 5 McGiven Drive, New Plymouth, RD1 New Zealand; in SOUTH AFRICA by Rolf C. Hagen S.A. (PTY.) LTD., P.O. Box 201199, Durban North 4016, South Africa; in JAPAN by T.F.H. Publications, Japan—Jiro Tsuda, 10-12-3 Ohjidai, Sakura, Chiba 285, Japan. Published by T.F.H. Publications, Inc.
MANUFACTURED IN THE
UNITED STATES OF AMERICA
BY T.F.H. PUBLICATIONS, INC.

HISTORY OF THE BIRMAN

Although some may expect the Burmese to be the sacred cat of Burma, that honor goes to the Birman. In fact, the word *Birman* is derived from the French spelling of Burma, "Birmanie," because it was the French who first introduced the Birman to the cat fancy.

The Birman's beginnings are shrouded in the kind of legend and mystery that delight cat fanciers of all ages. The folk tale describing how the Birman obtained its unique coloring and markings offers explanations where real history and accurate records leave us guessing.

Before the time when Christ walked the earth, and even before the time of Buddha, an ancient people called the Khmer lived in a southeast Asian country once called Burma and now called Myanmar. The Khmer believed in the magical ability of animals to ward off malevolence and evil forces.

In the temple of Lao-Tsun on the slopes of the Lugh, there lived 100 golden-eyed temple cats with long white hair. The cats bore the

Although the history of the Birman is unclear, it has not affected the popularity of the breed.

Birmans are known for their brilliant blue eyes and luxurious coats. This trio of white, fluffy kittens is hard to resist.

souls of the Kittah, or Khmer priests, after they had departed this life and awaited rebirth as the high priest in order to attain purity and perfection.

In the temple lived the golden-bearded Grand Lama of all the Kittah. His entire life was devoted to worshipping Tsun-Kyan-Kse, the goddess in the golden robes with brilliant blue eyes who presided over the transformation of priestly souls as they left one life and entered the next.

One clear evening, the honorable Mun Ha sat before the goddess in prayer. Next to him sat his devoted cat, Sinh, who was one of the white cats that resided in the temple. Like the other temple cats, Sinh had eyes that were as golden as the robes of the goddess and his ears, nose, tail, and tips of his feet were as dark

as the color of earth, a symbol of the impurity of all that touches the ground.

That evening, as Mun Ha prayed, invaders from Siam, the land that is now called Thailand, entered the temple, killing Mun Ha on his throne. Because Mun Ha could no longer direct his gaze to the eternal goddess, Sinh put his paws on his noble master and faced the statue of Tsun Kyan-Kse. As Sinh contemplated the goddess, a miraculous transformation took place. As the other Kittah that had gathered around Mun Ha watched, Sinh's hair turned the color of a golden mist that matched the color of Tsun Kyan-Kse's robes. His eyes became the same blazing sapphire blue as those of the goddess, and his paws became pure white to the point where

Above: According to an ancient legend, Birmans acquired their blue eyes and white feet from Kyan-Kse, the goddess in the golden robes.

Below: Birmans are a popular choice among cat lovers because of the breed's moderate demeanor, easy-to-maintain coat, and adorable face.

they were covered by his master's holy garments. As Sinh faced the entrance to the temple, his gaze turned to the bronze doors. When the Kittahs realized the meaning of Sinh's gaze, they rushed to the doors and closed them, thus saving the temple from being plundered by the invaders from Siam.

Sinh continued to sit on Mun Ha's throne for seven days contemplating Tsun Kyan-Kse. On the seventh day he died, taking the pure and perfect soul of his master with him. Seven days thereafter, the Kittah assembled in front of Tsun Kyan-Kse's statue to select Mun Ha's successor. All of the temple cats gathered there with them. As the

priests prayed, the hair of the cats turned a golden color as Sinh's had done. Their eyes became the brilliant blue of the goddess, and the paws on all four feet turned pure white. Silently, the cats that possessed the souls of the temple's departed Kittah, gathered around the youngest Kittah and chose him as Mun Ha's successor. From that day forward, the sacred cats of Burma had coats of a golden mist, eyes of sapphire blue, and feet as pure and white as new-fallen snow.

Recorded history of the Birman's beginnings is not so detailed, decidedly less clear, and certainly less romantic. Among the cats suspected of being responsible for the Birman's origin are Siamese and long-haired, bicolored Angoras that carried the genes for point color, white spotting, and long hair.

Several stories surround the Birman's introduction into western culture and subsequently the cat fancy. As a gesture of thanks for his help in saving the sacred temple of Lao Tsun during an uprising in the early part of the 20th century, monks gave two Birman cats to Major Gordon Russell, an officer of the British army then serving in Burma. The cats were shipped to France to Russell and another gentleman, August Pavie. The male, named Maldepour, died enroute. The female, a pregnant cat named Sita, found her way to France in 1919. Her offspring started the Birman line in the West. A second account relates that the cats were stolen by greedy temple servants who traded

The Siamese and the long-haired, bicolored Angora are suspected of being responsible for the Birman's origin. Both breeds carried the genes for point color, white spotting, and long hair.

them for gold. The third story claims that the cats were imported into France in 1925 by a Madame Marcelle Adam. Regardless of which account one believes, the Birman was introduced into France in the early part of the 20th century, into the French cat fancy shortly thereafter, and into the hearts of breeders and cat lovers in Britain and the United States decades later. The French cat registry recognized the Birman as a separate breed in 1925 and named it Sacre de Birmanie. It wasn't until 1966 that the breed received recognition in England, and it was 1967 before the Cat Fanciers Association (CFA) recognized it in the US.

The Sacred Cat of Burma Fanciers is the oldest Birman breed club in the Cat Fanciers' Association.

Upon her introduction, the Birman was cherished in France, and it is the French who are credited with preserving the Birman line during World War II when its breeding numbers dwindled. Outcrossing with Persians and Himalayans helped ensure the Birman's survival during that time.

Birmans first arrived in the United States in 1959. Today, most American Birmans can be traced to England, France, and Australia. Imported cats expand the gene pool and the point color possibilities. Birmans are popular among the purebred cat-owning public because of their moderate types, easy-to-maintain coats, and pleasing faces that are not extreme in any way.

There are two national Birman organizations to which breeders can belong. One is the Sacred Cat of Burma Fanciers, which is the oldest Birman breed club in the Cat Fanciers' Association. The club produces a newsletter for its members and hosts an annual cat show. The other national organization is the National Birman Fanciers, also affiliated with CFA, which holds an annual show in New Jersey. Both organizations celebrate the Birman for breeders throughout the United States.

BIRMAN CHARACTER

Among the many breeds of cats, Birmans stand out as being extremely sociable, trusting, and domesticated. Breeders and owners describe them as gentle, quiet, loving, companionable, and loyal. They have a very gracious and noble demeanor and love being with people. Although they may bond with one member of the family more than another, they are not necessarily one-person cats. If one person is not available to pet them, they will go to someone who is. Some Birmans want to be lap cats, some prefer to be on an arm of a chair next to you, but all of them want to be around their people.

Birmans are always there when you need them—mellow, friendly, and moderately active. In fact, "moderate" is another word used often to describe the Birman: playful, but not rambunctious; active, but not mischievous; desirous of attention, but not demanding; social, but not the center of attention. You will never find a Birman climbing your curtains or rocketing to the top of a door, although some of them do like to sit on top of a bookcase to observe the world beneath them.

One of their special qualities is the eye contact that they maintain with their owners. A Birman will look you right in the eyes as a way of displaying her affection and capture your heart with her soulful gaze. Quietly speak her name and watch your

Birmans are gentle and loving companions that enjoy spending time with their people. It's important that you take the time to form a long-lasting friendship with your Birman.

Although Birmans are active and playful, they do not need to be the center of attention. These two Birmans enjoy an afternoon lounging around.

Birman slowly close both eyes and open them again, which is an action equal to blowing your Birman a kiss from across the room.

Expect your Birman to be an individual in some ways, too. Although the cats will be affectionate, they can be at times preoccupied. When they want attention, Birmans will wrap you around their paws and make you pet them or provide them with what they want.

If you are sensitive and like to spend time with a good friend and value the beauty and heritage of this fanciful feline, then the Birman is for you. However, don't be away from home too often or too long unless you have a cat companion for your Birman, because these cats like company. Birmans are polite and don't tend to be demanding, but they need love and attention to be truly happy cats. If you are a senior citizen, you will find the Birman's gentle, well-behaved ways make it an excellent pet.

ALL IN THE FAMILY

In terms of personality, Birmans are more often compared to dogs than cats. In multicat environments, they are social and pack oriented. For this reason, Birmans make great pets in a family where one person loves cats and the other prefers dogs. If you have a spouse who would prefer a Fido to a Fluffy, expect him or her to be converted by the magical charms, gentle disposition, and loving ways of the Birman.

Birmans like to be with their human families in the middle of any family activity. Because Birmans are patient, kind, and very even tempered, they are a good choice for families with children. They are extremely tolerant of children and younger family members and adjust well to their humans' busy lives. If they need a break when activities become a little hectic, expect them to simply disappear and get away from it all.

Because of their sweet demeanor, Birmans are an excellent choice for families with children. They are extremely tolerant of young children and can adapt to any situation.

If you have young children, they should be taught to treat the cats with respect and to handle them gently. Cats are living creatures, not stuffed animals, and they need to be handled with care and allowed to have their own time and space when they want it.

If you have other pets, your Birman will fit right in with your menagerie. They are not high-strung nor are they afraid of other animals. They will coexist well with dogs, other cats, and even birds. Instead of waiting in hiding to pounce on your dog, you may find your Birman cultivating a relationship by rubbing against him or see both engaged in mutual grooming.

Like all kittens, Birmans are playful and mischievous. However, they are generally quiet and not overly rambunctious like some of the more wiry breeds.

BIRMAN KITTENS

Birman kittens are playful, but generally quiet and not rambunctious like the more wiry breeds, such as the Siamese. They are active, constantly inquisitive, and quick to learn. Birmans quickly develop trust and bond to the other kittens in the litter. They will readily run and chase each other or the safe toys that you provide. When you are busy with tasks that need your attention, your Birman kitten will find activities to amuse herself.

Birman kittens also love to be cuddled and to snuggle. They are apt to crawl into tight, unexpected places to sleep if your lap isn't readily available, so keep potentially dangerous places such as open clothes dryers off limits.

BIRMAN ADULTS

Because of their outgoing nature, Birmans develop good social skills. Don't expect your Birman to hide under the bed when someone comes to visit because Birmans love company and run to the door when the doorbell rings to see who it is. In fact, your Birman may think the company came especially to see her and plop down on some stranger's lap.

Adult Birmans are more sedate than kittens, but they still want to play and be around their human companions every day. Your Birman will like to be involved in all of the human activities in your house, even if it means lying on a newspaper or book that you are reading or supervising your activities while you are making dinner.

Snuggling is what some of them like to do best, so expect your Birman to want to share your bed at night by burrowing under the covers to get warm or sleeping on the pillow next to you. Although some Birmans are not lap cats, they usually like to be within touching distance of you, whether they are sitting near you on the arm of the sofa as you watch television or simply following you from room to room to see what you are doing. You seldom have to wonder where your Birman is.

PLAYTIME

Birmans like to play with you, so their most favorite toys will be the ones that require you at the other end. Younger Birmans will

Keep your Birman occupied with fun and interesting toys, such as sparkly toys and pom-poms.

What could be better than a room full of Birmans? Because of her outgoing personality, expect your Birman to be involved in all the family activities.

play alone, but as they get older, they really like you to entertain them. When your Birman gets the morning and evening crazies, she may seem like a member of the flying Wolendas as she runs around the house for a few moments. Then she goes back to being her quiet, dignified self.

Birmans love to chase things that you throw, and in keeping with their dog-like personalities, sometimes learn to fetch. A favorite game you can play with your Birman is shining a laser light or flashlight on the floors and walls and watch her try to catch the spot of light as it bounces around. Your Birman will like interactive toys, such as Mylar sparkly toys on a plastic stick, fishing pole toys, sparkle balls, pom-poms, and catnip toys of all kinds. Your Birman may clutch her catnip toys and kick them with her back feet

like an object of prey. Remember that the more you play with your kitten, the more she will want to play as an adult.

STRONG, SILENT TYPE

Birmans are relatively quiet in the realm of cat-speak. Some have a squeaky voice, but most are soft-spoken and refined. However, if they want something they have no problem letting you know, but even when they do vocalize, their voices are fairly quiet. When engaging in a favorite feline activity—bird watching—Birmans will make a little chirping or clicking noise as most other cats do. When they want to be left alone, they may depart in a huff, as if to say, "I'm tired of this activity and need time to myself." Don't be put off. Your Birman will want you to interact again as soon as she spends a little time by herself.

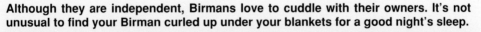

Although they are independent, Birmans love to cuddle with their owners. It's not unusual to find your Birman curled up under your blankets for a good night's sleep.

THE BIRMAN STANDARD AND COLORS

The Birman is a cat with a look as ethereal as described in her legendary history. She is a strongly built cat and has a long and stocky body. An adult Birman may weigh from 8 to 12 pounds, with females proportionately smaller than males. Birmans are covered with a coat of silky white or ivory-colored hair that develops a golden mist—or faint beige cast—as they age. The hair on the legs, tail, face, and ears, called points, is darker than that of the body coat. The Birman's face and muzzle are round, with strong jaws and a firm chin. Her ears are set apart as much to the side of the head as to the top of the head and are proportional to her size. Birman eyes are a deep blue. They should be set wide apart and appear almost round, creating a sweet, alluring expression.

According to the standard, Birmans are strongly built, with long, lean bodies. Their luxurious coats and blazing blue eyes set them apart from other breeds.

Characteristic to a Birman are the white feet. While most pet owners refer to a cat's white feet as mittens or boots, in the Birman these markings are called gloves on the front feet and laces on the hind feet. Judges look for symmetry and height of the front gloves on each foot, and it is gloving irregularities, such as too much or too little white, that often relegate a Birman to the status of pet quality rather than show quality. The laces should extend one-half to three-quarters up the back of the hind legs ending in a point or inverted "V."

THE STANDARD

Anyone who has watched an Olympic gymnastics meet or skating competition knows that competitors have a standard against which their performances are judged. Likewise, cats entering show competitions are evaluated against a breed standard that has been established by the association in which they are registered. Simply stated, breed standards are ideals of appearance against which each cat is judged. The winning cat in each category should most closely match the standard for its breed.

If you have a pet-quality Birman, it will provide you with the same love and companionship as a show-quality one, but if you are planning to compete in cat shows, it is best to familiarize yourself with the standard for the breed and learn to recognize an outstanding specimen.

Each cat registry applies a certain number of points to each of the various bodily features

A somewhat mysterious cat, the Birman has a distinctive appearance, complete with long, silky hair, four pure white feet, and piercing blue eyes.

based on their relative importance. Judges, however, don't mentally add up the points for each cat in the show ring as they are judging. Rather, they look for features that don't conform to breed standards and that might disqualify a cat.

The Birman standards may vary slightly from registry to registry. Unlike the dog fancy, which is regulated exclusively by the American Kennel Club, the cat fancy has more than six US and Canadian registries that track the lineage or pedigree of the members' cats. The largest registry in the world is the Cat Fanciers Association, Inc. (CFA) and it is the CFA standard that is reproduced here with kind permission.

POINT SCORE

HEAD, BODY, TYPE & COAT (65)

Head (including boning, nose, jaw, chin profile, ear and eye shape and set.)......30

Body/Type (including boning, stockiness elongation, legs, tail.)......25

NOSE
Medium in length and width

EYES
Round

HEAD
Skull strong, broad, and rounded

EARS
Medium in length

CHIN
Strong and well developed

CHEEKS
Full

JAW
Heavy

LEGS
Medium in length

TAIL
Medium in length

PAWS
Large, round, and firm

Coat (including length, texture, ruff.)......10

COLOR— INCLUDING EYE COLOR (35)

Color except gloves (including body color, point color, eye color.)......15

Gloves (including front & rear gloves, laces and symmetry)......20

GENERAL: A cat of mystery and legend, the Birman is a color-pointed cat with long silky hair and four pure white feet. She is strongly built, elongated and stocky, neither svelte nor cobby. The distinctive head has strong jaws, firm chin, medium-length Roman nose with nostrils set low on the nose leather. There should be good width between the ears, which are medium in size. The blue, almost round eyes are set well apart, giving a sweet expression to the face.

HEAD: skull strong, broad, and rounded. There is a slight flat spot just in front of the ears.

"Tennessee Moon" is the perfect example of a lilac point male. According to the standard, the lilac point is almost white with frosty grey points.

NOSE: medium in length and width, in proportion to size of head.

Roman shape in profile. Nostrils set low on the nose leather.

PROFILE: The forehead slopes back and is slightly convex. The medium-length nose, which starts just below the eyes, is Roman in shape (which is slightly convex), with the nostrils set low on the nose leather. The chin is strong, with the lower jaw forming a perpendicular line with the upper lip.

CHEEKS: full with somewhat rounded muzzle. The fur is short about the face, but the fur is longer to the extreme outer area of the cheek.

JAWS: heavy.

CHIN: strong and well-developed.

EARS: medium in length. Almost as wide at the base as tall. Modified to a rounded point at the tip; set as much to the side as into the top of the head.

EYES: almost round with a sweet expression. Set well apart, with the outer corner tilted VERY slightly upward. Blue in color, the deeper the blue the better.

BODY: long and stocky. Females may be proportionately smaller than males.

LEGS: medium in length and heavy.

PAWS: large, round, and firm. Five toes in front, four behind.

TAIL: medium in length, in pleasing proportion to the body.

COAT: medium long to long, silken in texture, with heavy ruff around the neck, slightly curly on stomach. This fur is of such a texture that it does not mat.

This mother cat and her baby share the same brilliant blue eyes that Birmans are so well known for.

COLOR EXCEPT GLOVES:
Body: even, with subtle shading when allowed. Strong contrast between body color and points. **Points except gloves**: mask, ears, legs, and tail dense and clearly defined, all of the same shade. Mask covers entire face including whisker pads and is connected to ears by tracings. No ticking or white hair in points. **Golden Mist**: desirable in all points colors is the "golden mist," a faint golden beige cast on the back and sides. This is somewhat deeper in the seal points, and may be absent in kittens.

GLOVES: **Front paws**: front paws have white gloves ending in an even line across the paw at, or between, the second or third joints. (The third joint is where the paw bends when the cat is standing.) The upper limit of white should be the metacarpal (dew) pad. (The metacarpal pad is the highest-up little paw pad,

located in the middle of the back of the front paw, above the third joint and just below the wrist bones.) Symmetry of the front gloves is desirable. **Back paws**: white glove covers all the toes, and may extend up somewhat higher than front gloves. Symmetry of the rear gloves is desirable. **Laces**: the gloves on the back paws must extend up the back of the hock, and are called laces in this area. Ideally, the laces end in a point or inverted "V" and extend one-half to three-fourths of the way up the hock. Lower or higher laces are acceptable, but should not go beyond the hock. Symmetry of the two laces is desirable. **Paw pads**: pink preferred, but dark spot(s) on paw pad(s) acceptable because of the two colors in pattern. **Note**: ideally, the front gloves match, the back gloves match, and the two laces match. Faultlessly gloved cats are a rare exception, and the Birman is to be judged in all its parts, as well as the gloves.

PENALIZE: white that does not run across the front paws in an even line. Persian or Siamese type head. Delicate bone structure. White shading on stomach and chest. Lack of laces on one or both back gloves. White beyond the metacarpal (dew) pad. (The metacarpal pad is the highest-up little paw pad, located in the middle of the back of the front paw, above the third joint and just below the wrist bones.)

DISQUALIFY: lack of white gloves on any paw. Kinked or abnormal tail. Crossed eyes. Incorrect number of toes. Areas of pure white in the points, if not connected to the gloves and part of or an extension of the gloves. Paw pads are part of the gloves. Areas of white connected to other areas of white by paw pads (of any color) are not a cause for disqualification.

Discrete areas of point color in the gloves, if not connected to point color of legs (exception, paw pads). White on back legs beyond the hock.

BIRMAN COLORS

Four colors are recognized by the CFA. The seal point body is an even pale fawn to cream, warm in tone, shading gradually to lighter color on the stomach and chest. Points, except for gloves, are deep seal brown. Gloves pure white. Nose leather is the same color as points. Paw pads are pink.

The blue-point body is bluish white to pale ivory, shading gradually to almost white on stomach and chest. Points, except for gloves, are deep blue. Gloves are pure white. Nose leather is slate color. Paw pads are pink.

The chocolate-point body is ivory with no shading. Points, except for gloves, are a milk chocolate color, warm in tone. Gloves are pure white. Nose leather is cinnamon pink. Paw pads are pink.

The lilac point is almost white. Points, except for gloves, are frosty grey with pinkish tone. Gloves are pure white. Nose leather is lavender-pink. Paw pads are pink.

On all four color types, the eye color is blue, the deeper and more violet, the better.

Birman breeders have begun experimenting with other point colors such as tabby, or lynx, point, and red point, but not all registries accept them for championship status.

This pretty blue point female is "Madison." The blue point body is bluish white to pale ivory with deep blue points.

SELECTING A BIRMAN

Now that you've decided that the lovely, long-haired Birman is the cat for you, your next step is to make some decisions about what kind of Birman you want. A little bit of planning will go a long way in helping you find a cat suitable to your personal preferences and keep you from making any costly mistakes that you may later regret. Although their popularity has increased over the years, Birmans are still relatively uncommon among the many breeds of cats. If you want to adopt one, you may have to travel to another state to find one available, choose one by looking at breeder photographs, or perhaps even agree to be put on a waiting list. Even though the Birman's silky, mat-free coat is often referred to as "wash and wear," don't expect it to be maintenance free. Birmans still require regular grooming to maintain good coat condition.

KITTEN OR CAT

The first decision you should make is what age of cat do you want. People love kittens. They

Before purchasing a Birman, you should be aware of the breed's specific needs, such as grooming. Birmans require regular grooming to maintain their coats.

are playful, inquisitive, and fun to watch. Kittens are thought to come with no bad habits and no retraining requirements. Even so, the downside to adopting a kitten is that because your home is her playground, she will require more constant attention and energy than an older, more mature adult cat.

The adult cat, on the other hand, is one whose appearance and personality are developed. When you purchase an adult cat, what you see is what you get. No guesswork is involved in determining how the cat will turn out. If you are interested in exhibiting, the quality and conformation to the breed standard of an adult Birman will be apparent. For the potential exhibitor, purchasing an adult that has competed in the ring a few times will help simplify the process of finding a show cat.

If simply finding a healthy companion animal is your primary concern, an adult will offer the same love and affection as a kitten. Breeders often sell as pets adult cats that are no longer part of the show circuit or their breeding program, occasionally at a lower price than a kitten. The disadvantages to purchasing an adult cat are that you will not be able to shape her character and personality or watch her grow up. Although the cattery environment

Although Birman kittens are adorable little balls of fluff, they require a lot of work. An adult Birman might be a better choice for some people.

Birmans love to be showered with love and affection. This happy pair has fun just fooling around.

will play an important part in a cat's ability to adjust to a new home, an adult cat may take longer to adjust than a kitten.

MALE OR FEMALE

Generalizing about differences in the sexes of felines can be as puzzling as generalizing about human males and females. Just when you think you have a rule of thumb, someone comes along and points to an exception. Given an environment filled with love and affection, both male and female cats make great pets.

If you are planning to become a breeder, finding a top-quality female should be your primary concern. Stud service can be provided by a male under contract from another cattery.

Intact male cats engage in territorial spray markings that result in a characteristic cat odor that is offensive and difficult to eliminate. Thus, keeping a male that is not neutered in your home can cause problems that you may not want to address, unless you are committed to becoming a breeder, or if you can find a separate location in your home in which to maintain the cat.

The sex you choose will ultimately be a matter of personal preference. Breeders say male cats tend to be affectionate lap cats that can be depended on to seek out their owners consistently for petting sessions or attention, once a bond of trust is established.

While just as affectionate, a female might want your attention one minute and be rather quiet the next. Your cat, no doubt, will be the exception to the rule. As a general rule, male Birmans are larger in size than the females, sometimes reaching 12 or more pounds.

Although Birmans are affectionate by nature, breeders say that males tend to be more so than females. Males are also larger in size than the females, sometimes reaching 12 or more pounds.

PET OR SHOW

The vast majority of kittens available for purchase, even from reputable breeders, are commonly referred to as pet-quality kittens, i.e., those that do not conform to breed standards in some way. The lack of conformation may simply mean that a Birman's gloves are uneven or the laces are too long. Don't be misled into thinking that a pet-quality kitten is in some way substandard or that

There are no major differences between male and female Birmans. Both sexes make wonderful pets and companions.

A Birman kitten's gloving begins at two to four weeks of age, and a pattern called a white blaze then appears above the nose. This mother cat takes excellent care of her babies.

if you purchase one, her life will be full of health-related problems. A cat's lack of conformation will only be a problem if you intend to exhibit your cat, in which case, the more closely she conforms to the standard, the better chance you have of successfully competing.

Most Birman breeders keep their kittens until they are 12 to 16 weeks of age. During that time, they are able to judge the kittens and determine which ones may make the best show cats. Birman kittens are born white and develop their coloring through the first four months of life. The tipping begins at one to two weeks of age on the ear tips and nose leather. At two to four weeks of age the white gloving begins and a pattern called a *white blaze* appears above the kitten's nose. It isn't until six to eight weeks that gloving can begin to be assessed. The evenness of the gloves is one of the criteria that determines whether the cat will be show quality or pet quality. At 12 to 16 weeks of age point color continues up the Birman kitten's legs, and her musculature becomes more noticeable. Gloving conformity will also be more apparent. Although a Birman is mature at 18 months, the cat continues to develop in size, bone structure, musculature, and coat into her third year of life.

Birman kittens are born white and develop their coloring during the first four months of life. These babies look like they're ready for the world, color or not.

Breeders typically keep the best quality kittens in a litter to be used for their own breeding programs, so purchasing a show-quality cat is more difficult than purchasing a pet-quality one. It's easier to determine whether a cat is show quality if she is older and has a proven history in the show ring. If showing or breeding is your intention, ask the breeder to show you the kitten's pedigree. Find out how many champions the sire and dam have produced and what titles other members of the family have accumulated. Ask to see cats with a proven track record.

ONE CAT OR TWO?

Because Birmans are very social cats and like companion–ship, you might want to consider purchasing two instead of one, especially if no one is home during the day or if you must be away from home periodically. You will have the easiest time bringing two cats into your home if they are littermates and purchased at the same time. If you decide to bring a second Birman into your home after purchasing the first, you can ensure a successful bonding by introducing the cats gradually. Keep the new cat separate for a few days and allow both cats to smell each other from behind closed doors. Allow the new cat to have access to the rest of the house for short periods of time. Gradually increase the amount of time until both felines are acclimated to one another.

WHERE TO BUY

Although you will be able to find kittens from an array of sources—pet shops, newspaper ads, breeders, and maybe even the person in the cubicle next to you at the office—it can't be stressed enough that finding a reputable breeder from which to purchase your Birman will help ensure that you find a healthy cat to be your companion for a long time. If showing or breeding Birmans is in your future, it is imperative that you find a reputable breeder from whom to buy a cat that is free of contagious diseases and conforms to the standard of the breed.

Pet shops care little about where their animals come from and where they go. Because responsible breeders want to make sure that their kittens are placed in good homes with people who can adequately care for them, they screen prospective buyers. Pet shops care only that the buyer has the money to pay for the kitten. Because responsible breeders often belong to clubs that have codes of ethics prohibiting members from selling kittens to pet shops, these shops are forced to rely on kitten and puppy mills—commercial kennels that churn out kittens and puppies simply to make a profit. Females live in cages and are kept pregnant whenever they are in heat, which can be three to four times a year. Because profit is the motive, little money is spent on veterinary care and adequate nutrition for the pregnant female or her offspring. You as the buyer will never see where the cat came from and what kind of conditions under which it was born and raised.

Pet shops also rely on the backyard breeder as supplier—the person who has a purebred

Birmans are very social cats and enjoy the company of their humans. If you have to leave your Birman home alone on a daily basis, you might want to think about purchasing another cat.

female cat and wants her, for whatever reason, to have a litter of kittens. Like the mills, backyard breeders care little about the health and well-being of the offspring and where they will be placed, much less whether the kittens conform to a breed standard.

To find reputable breeders, look in the directories of the major cat magazines. Most of the national registries offer breeder referral lines that will point you to breeders in your geographic area. There is a web site devoted specifically to Birmans at http://www.birman.com/ and it is a good place to get information and names of breeders. Ask your veterinarian if he or she is familiar with any breeders in your area. Look in the pet columns of your local newspapers. Contact a local cat club and attend a show to find not only breeders, but to see the kinds of cats they produce.

Once you have located some breeders, visit their catteries. Some registries, such as the CFA, have cattery inspection programs, which means that catteries have been inspected by veterinarians and adhere to specific standards. The program is voluntary, and breeders must pay an inspection fee to the veterinarian and a

Although you can find a kitten through various sources, such as newspapers or pet shops, contacting a reputable breeder ensures that you obtain a healthy and well-bred cat.

certification fee to CFA. The certification is good for one year from the time of inspection. You will learn a lot about the quality of the cats produced in a cattery just by visiting it and asking the breeder questions. Do the cats appear healthy? Do they appear to conform to the breed standard? Do the cats and kittens socialize with humans or do they stay in cages? During the first two to three weeks of life, a cat is at her most impressionable stage, and early socialization plays an important role in forming the companionable nature of a cat. It is during this time that the most important part of the socialization process takes place. Kittens left alone to amuse themselves will continue to do so as they become adults, whereas the kitten that experienced human contact as an important part of her life will continue to seek out that human contact as an adult. If the breeder is a good one, he or she will have provided the kittens with ample human contact that will help them adjust to life as companions.

It's important to ask a breeder many questions when visiting a cattery. You want to make sure that the breeder is responsible and cares about the well-being of his or her cats.

What are the conditions under which the queen and her offspring are kept? Are pregnant females and kittens given food that meets the special nutritional requirements of their condition and age?

Expect the breeder to ask questions of you, too. Good breeders invest a lot of time, effort, and money in their cats and kittens and will want to know if you can continue to provide them with excellent care. You also will be required to sign a contract at the time of purchase, which will require you to spay or neuter the cat you purchase unless it is for a legitimate breeding program.

If the nearest cattery is too far away to visit, ask the breeder to send you photos of the kittens available. Most breeders will ship a kitten to you if you cannot come to get her. Regardless of the cattery's location, ask the breeder to give you references. People who have purchased kittens or cats from the breeder will be able to offer you insight into the relative quality of the cats they bought.

Early spaying and neutering is growing in acceptance. Some breeders are having their cats altered at the age of 16 weeks, at which time they make them available for placement. You may be able to find a Birman that has already had this important surgery.

A HEALTHY CAT

If the breeder is a good one, you can be sure of obtaining a healthy cat. By the time a kitten is offered for sale, she has been weaned, is eating solid food, has received her first set of vaccinations, and has visited a veterinarian at least once. Cattery animals are routinely tested for contagious diseases. Reputable breeders offer a health guarantee that the purchased animal will remain healthy for a specified time period after purchase, and if the kitten falls ill, she will be replaced or the money refunded.

Healthy kittens and cats are alert. Their eyes are bright, shiny, and clear, with no watery discharge. Their ears are clean and free of dirt. Their coats have no bald patches or evidence of flea dirt, and the area around their tails should be clean.

Bright, shiny eyes, clean ears, and luxurious coats are signs of a healthy and well-adjusted cat. This pretty kitty is no exception.

GENERAL CARE AND GROOMING

Before bringing your Birman home, you will need to purchase some items that are basic necessities. A litter box should be first on your list. Litter boxes come in all shapes and sizes. Even if your Birman is a kitten or small adult, a larger litter box is better because it will provide the cat ample room to turn around and dig—a feline favorite pastime—and prevent you from having to invest in a larger box as your cat grows. If your home or apartment is small, you might want to buy a covered box or one of the newer litter boxes concealed in a piece of furniture. If your local pet store does not carry the kind of box you want, check in the classified sections of the major cat magazines at the newsstand.

A litter box should be one of the first things that you purchase before bringing your Birman kitten home. A large litter box will not only provide your Birman with a lot of space, but it will prevent you from having to buy another one as she grows.

You'll find just as many types of cat box filler as you will litter boxes. Whether clay or clumping, litter can be made from newspaper pellets, corn cobs, or wood chips. Some filler requires disposal with the rest of your garbage, while other types can be flushed down the toilet. Cats seem to develop preferences for certain types of litter. Perhaps one is less dusty or softer on their feet. When you purchase your Birman, find out from the breeder what kind of litter she is accustomed to, then make any changes gradually to keep litter box aversion problems from occurring.

Cats are naturally drawn to anything that they can dig and bury their wastes in, so your Birman kitten will know already how to use the box when you purchase it. To help your new kitten or cat learn where the litter box is, show it to her immediately. Keeping the litter box clean is the best way to ensure that your cat continues to use it, so purchase a slotted litter scoop, and remove wastes daily.

In addition to digging, scratching is another favorite feline occupation. Scratching enables cats to remove the sheaths of their nails as the new nail grows in and to mark objects with their scent using glands on the pads of their feet. Some cat owners have their cats declawed, a procedure whereby the toenails, usually on the front feet, are surgically removed. You may be under contract with the

All cats love to scratch because it enables them to remove the sheaths of their nails as the new nails grow in. Providing your Birman with a scratching post like this innovative "tree" will keep her occupied and happy.

breeder from whom you purchased your Birman not to have her declawed. If you intend to show your cat, her claws must be intact. Cats are as naturally drawn to scratch posts as they are to their litter boxes, so providing posts made of carpet, sisal rope, or wood is an effective way to save wear and tear on your furniture, and it is a safe, painless alternative to declawing.

Your Birman will spend up to 16 hours a day sleeping and may want to snuggle with you when you hit the sack. You might be flattered and encourage her to do so. Even if your cat has a welcome sleeping place in your bed, providing other sleeping areas around the house will help your cat feel at home and may help cat hair from accumulating on your furniture. Cats love to sleep in tight, cozy

Don't be alarmed if your new kitten sleeps the day away. A kitten can spend up to 16 hours a day sleeping, so make sure that you have a nice warm bed for her to curl up in.

places. Fake fur kitty cups and molded beds enable your cat to curl up inside for a good night's sleep or a quick catnap. Soft foam beds that can be placed on a chair or sofa keep your cat's spirits up and cat hair deposits down. Beds can be as simple as a fabric-covered piece of foam or as elaborate as a double-decker bunk bed. You will find them in various colors to match any decor.

Food and water bowls come in glass, aluminum, plastic, ceramic, and china. Plastic has an advantage in that it won't break, but plastic accumulates oils that are difficult to remove and may exacerbate a case of feline acne—black, crusty patches on a cat's chin. If you purchase ceramic or china

bowls, make certain that they are lead free. Because cats don't typically drink water with their meals, avoid combination bowls that have food and water sections joined together. Place your cat's water dish away from her food bowl in another part of the kitchen or in another room altogether to encourage drinking.

Playtime will be an important part of your interaction with your Birman. Provide her with safe toys to occupy her time with or without you. Interactive toys enable a cat to exercise and have fun. Toys need not be expensive, either. A cat will enjoy chasing a crumpled piece of paper or sliding in a paper sack with no handles as much as playing with a more costly, complex apparatus.

SAFETY

Keeping your cat indoors will prevent certain accidents from happening, but your home is not totally safe unless you take the necessary precautions. Many houseplants are poisonous to cats. Ingesting them can cause symptoms that range from stomach upset and vomiting to coma and death. The list of poisonous plants is extensive, so ask your veterinarian for one and eliminate any from your home or place them out of your cat's reach. To provide your cat with a fresh supply of greens, plant some grass seed in a small container for her to chew.

Keep harmful chemicals and medicines out of your cat's reach. Mothballs, cleansers, cleaning products, or human prescription or non-prescription drugs can be fatal to the cat that swallows them. When cleaning, remove any residue of the cleaning product to prevent your Birman from getting any on her coat then licking it off. Cats are drawn to antifreeze, so clean up any that has spilled in your garage. Antifreeze with propylene glycol instead of ethylene glycol is safer, but it is still toxic if enough is ingested.

Tie up loose electrical chords if your cat seems to want to chew on them. Don't allow miniblind cords or drapery pulls

Food and water bowls come in glass, aluminum, plastic, ceramic, and china. It's important to clean the bowl after each meal to prevent bacteria from forming and potentially harming your cat.

Cats are known to climb up onto countertops and windowsills to investigate their surroundings. Keep anything harmful out of your cat's reach.

to dangle and entice your kitten or cat to play and thereby accidentally get caught in them. Keep small objects, such as needles, pins, coins, and paper clips out of sight and out of mind.

GROOMING

Birmans have coats that are medium long to long, silken in texture, with a heavy ruff around their necks and slightly curly hair on their stomachs. The hair is of such a texture that it does not mat, and consequently, Birmans are frequently referred to as "wash-and-wear" cats. Even so, you will need to groom your Birman regularly, including giving her a periodic bath. Since cats love to wash themselves, you may wonder why that is necessary. Grooming will help keep loose hair to a minimum and help prevent your cat from getting hairballs—wads of swallowed hair that form clumps that a cat expels by vomiting. These clumps can become lodged in the digestive tract and cause blockage. Grooming will help you detect any fleas and discover skin problems or bald patches caused by allergic reactions.

Birmans love to be groomed, and you may find yours lying on her back with her paws over her head, making it easy to comb her belly. Train cats at a young to accept the grooming routine.

Basic Birman grooming tools include a long-toothed metal comb with the teeth relatively far apart, cat toothbrush and toothpaste, cat shampoo, and nail clippers. Combining home health exams with weekly grooming sessions are a good way to keep apprised of your cat's physical condition.

Comb your Birman's hair weekly with the metal comb. Your Birman may keep her nails trimmed by scratching them on the post you've provided, but if you are entering a cat show, you will be required to clip the nails on all four paws. Before bathing your cat, use a nail clipper specifically made for trimming cats' nails. Hold your cat's paw, spread her toes, and look at the nails. You will notice that each has a pink area closer to the nail base. This is called the "quick." When you trim the nails, it is extremely important not to trim the quick. Trimming into the quick is extremely painful to a cat and can cause the nail to bleed.

Once your cat's nails are trimmed, move on to the bath. Cats often demonstrate an aversion to bathing, but if you are planning to exhibit your Birman, you will need to bathe and groom her prior to each show. The sooner you begin getting her accustomed to bathing, the better off both of you will be. A bath every three to four months will help your Birman maintain good coat condition when you are not entering her into a show. During

One of the basic grooming tools includes a long-toothed metal brush. Comb your Birman's hair on a weekly basis to keep her coat in good condition.

the process, relax and make the experience a positive one for your kitten. When bathing her, use only a mild shampoo intended for use on cats and kittens. Make sure the room temperature is warm enough for your kitten during her bath and afterward when you towel her dry. Have clean towels handy. Fill a sink or small dishpan with warm water. If you like, put a bath mat on the bottom of the container so your kitten won't slide. Allow your kitten to get used to standing in the water. You might want to just go this far a few times before you actually wash her. When you are applying shampoo and working up a lather, keep it out of your kitten's eyes and ears. Use a washcloth on her face and make sure you wash between your cat's toes and also the hindquarters. Thoroughly dry your cat with a blow dryer or a drying cage.

If you like, use a cream rinse or conditioner on your cat after her bath. These products will keep her hair silky and help prevent dryness. Use only products intended for use on cats. Products intended for people and for dogs can be toxic to your cat.

A thorough teeth cleaning should be included in your cat's annual checkup, but you will need to help in between times. Your veterinarian will be able to supply you with a toothbrush and toothpaste intended for cats. Use it regularly, and before a show, to contribute to a cat's overall health and well-being.

Bathing your Birman every three to four months will help maintain a good coat. Beginning the process at an early age will help make it a more positive experience.

Even though Birmans are referred to as "wash-and-wear" cats, they need to be groomed on a regular basis. Grooming your Birman will help keep loose hair to a minimum and prevent her from getting hairballs.

FEEDING BIRMANS

Up until the age of six to eight weeks, a cat's nutritional requirements are met by her mother. Once a kitten is weaned, it becomes the responsibility of the human caregiver to provide her with a nutritional diet to ensure growth into a healthy, happy adult and to maintain her health through the remaining stages of her life. Cats have a reputation for being finicky eaters and what may turn on the taste buds of one feline may, in fact, turn up the nose of another. Given all of the choices of commercial and premium cat food these days, it should be relatively easy for you to find a variety of foods to keep your Birman healthy and happy.

The standards by which pet food is tested and how pet food is labeled are regulated by the Association of American Feed Control Officials (AAFCO) who determine not only what goes on a label but the order in which it is presented. Reading the labels on cat foods can be confusing, but it is the best way to determine whether the food meets the stringent standards set up to provide your cat with

As a responsible pet owner, it's your job to feed your kitten the proper vitamins and nutrients necessary for healthy growth.

A cat's diet should include protein, water, carbohydrates for energy, dietary fat, vitamins, and minerals. Unlike humans, cats cannot exist solely on a vegetarian diet that contains protein from non-meat sources.

optimum nutrition. Cat food that is complete and nutritionally balanced will have a guarantee on the label that reads, "Animal feeding tests using AAFCO procedures substantiate that (brand name) provides complete and balanced nutrition for all life stages of cats."

NUTRIENTS

Just like you, cats need certain nutrients to maintain their body systems: protein, water, carbohydrates for energy, dietary fat, vitamins, and minerals. However, unlike humans who can exist on a vegetarian diet that contains protein only from non-meat sources, the cat has a digestive system that requires protein found in animal sources for optimum health. Cats are carnivores as a result of tens of thousands of years of evolution.

Because of their unique metabolisms, they require from two to three times the digestible protein of their canine counterparts. Good-quality commercial food will state on the package that it contains as the primary ingredients protein from meat, poultry, and by-products, or from seafood sources.

Protein is the source of amino acids, which are a major component of body tissue. One of the essential amino acids, taurine, has received much attention in recent years because lack of it can result in feline heart and eye problems. Most commercial foods now have taurine added to the product.

Like all mammals, cats require water to facilitate all of their bodily processes. Cats satisfy some of their water requirements through the food they eat. More water is found in canned (or wet) cat food than in dry, so a cat eating solely dry food will most likely consume more water than one eating a diet of wet food, or one that combines the wet and dry varieties.

Because today's domestic cat evolved from an ancestor that lived in the desert of northern Africa, it is able to withstand dehydration more than you or your pet dog. Normal bodily functions, such as urination, defecation, and perspiration cause your Birman to lose water that must be replaced. Provide fresh water daily. A freshly filled bowl somewhere other than next to your Birman's food dish will be a favorite watering hole. Some cats prefer their water cold, so you may find your Birman soliciting you to turn on the bathroom faucet or imploring you to share the jug of spring water in the refrigerator, rather than partake of water that is room temperature.

Carbohydrates in the form of sugars and starches are a source of energy that help a cat metabolize other nutrients and maintain body temperature, activity level, growth, and reproduction. Although your cat can obtain adequate amounts of energy from protein and fat, most commercial pet foods also contain carbohydrates.

The fat contained in cat food provides your Birman with energy and makes her food more palatable. Fat also supplies essential fatty acids that enable your cat to metabolize fat-soluble vitamins A, D, E, and K. Dietary fat will help your cat

Kittens need the proper care and guidance in order to mature into well-behaved, well-adjusted cats.

maintain a healthy, shiny coat, heal wounds, and fight infection.

Your Birman needs vitamins for metabolism of other nutrients and for growth and maintenance. Although too little vitamin content in a cat's diet can cause health problems, too much of certain vitamins can do the same. Water soluble vitamins, such as B complex, niacin, and thiamin are utilized and excess quantities eliminated. Amounts of vitamins A, D, E, and K that are not used immediately in the digestive process are stored in the body's

Treats can be provided on an occasional basis to help provide a little variety in the diet. Some treats act as a cleansing agent to help reduce tartar on a cat's teeth. Photo courtesy of Heinz.

The quantity of food that you feed your Birman is just as important as the food itself. A cat should not be so thin that her bones show, but if you cannot feel her ribs then she may have a weight problem.

fat. Because too much A and D can cause toxicity, veterinarians recommend that you not give your cat supplements unless you are advised to do so because of a health problem.

Your Birman requires minerals to aid in bone growth, tooth formation, blood clotting, basic metabolism, muscle function, anemia prevention, cell oxygenation, and proper functioning of the thyroid gland. Minerals work in combination with one another, and like the other essential nutrients, are present in quantities meeting recommended allowances in good commercial and premium cat foods.

TYPES OF FOOD

Thanks to a vast array of brands, cats can be treated to a variety of types of cat food. Although they differ in the way that they are processed by pet food manufacturers, all three types (wet, semi-moist, and dry) can provide adequate nutrition for your Birman. Read the labels carefully.

Wet—or canned—food is generally more expensive than the other types of cat food, but it is more palatable, especially if your cat is a finicky eater. Because it can contain more than 75 percent water, canned food is a good dietary source of this essential substance. Canned food is available in sizes from 2.5 ounces to 14 ounces. Although unopened cans have a lengthy shelf life, uneaten portions of such food must be refrigerated to maintain freshness.

Semi-moist cat food is less costly than canned but has more preservatives added to prevent spoilage of the product once the container has been opened. Many cat owners find semi-moist cat food more convenient because it can be kept for longer periods than canned food and can be freely fed to a cat without fear of it becoming contaminated as quickly as canned.

Dry is the most economical type of cat food. Because of its minimal water content, cats eat

Proper nutrition for your cat is always important. Your feline friend can reap the benefits of ultimate nutrition with healthy skin, a shiny coat, bright eyes, playful energy, and all-around good health. Photo courtesy of Nutro Products, Inc.

Provide your Birman with a variety of cat foods to prevent her from relying on one certain food that may not have the proper nutritional content.

less of it on an as-is basis than both the wet and semi-moist varieties. Dry food may be freely fed to a cat without the fear of it attracting insects or becoming rancid when exposed to the air. Chewing dry food also aids your Birman in keeping her teeth clean.

Regardless of the type of food you decide to feed your cat, variety is important to prevent her from relying on a food that may not be nutritionally complete. Protein should come from a mixture of meat, poultry, or fish to avoid deficiencies that might develop from consuming food from only one source—organ meats, red meat, or fish.

HOW MUCH TO FEED

The Birman has a muscular body, but size and weight may vary from cat to cat. You will want to feed a quantity that is appropriate for your particular cat. Many factors can affect the quantity of food your Birman requires on a daily basis: activity level, overall condition, age, and type of food, etc. An active kitten or young cat will require more calories than a less active adult or senior.

The bottom line is that your Birman's calorie intake should match her calorie expenditure. Counting calories for your cat can be as cumbersome and problematic as counting them for yourself, so using the following basic rule of thumb will help guide you in determining correct quantities. Every cat has a layer of subcutaneous fat, but you should be able to feel her rib cage beneath the skin. A cat should not be so thin that her bones show nor so fat that you cannot feel her ribs. If you can't feel the ribs, your Birman may be overweight and should be placed on a weight reduction program.

A cute, cuddly, and slightly plump kitten is adorable, but be sure to monitor your kitten's weight as she grows. Check the cat food labels for directions on how much to feed.

pet food products is the creation of types developed for cats of different ages. You will be able to find a wide variety of foods for kittens, adult cats, and seniors. If your Birman develops a health problem as she ages, such as feline lower urinary tract disease (LUTD) or kidney disease, discuss feeding options with your veterinarian. He or she will be able to recommend a food product to help your cat combat her illness.

Manufacturers offer on the labels guidelines for how much of their product to feed a cat. If you are feeding more than one type of food to your Birman, it will require less of each than the suggested quantity of each.

A more recent development in

Before bringing your Birman kitten or cat home, find out from the breeder or previous owner what she ate. If you want to alter her diet, do so gradually to prevent stress or dietary related problems, such as diarrhea, brought on by a sudden change in food.

HEALTH CARE

One of your primary respon–sibilities as a cat owner will be to provide your Birman kitten or cat with good veterinary medical care. Preventing problems before they start is always the best medicine, and annual veterinary checkups along with good nutrition will help you keep your Birman fit and healthy. A complete physical exam includes weighing your cat; examining her eyes, ears and mouth, teeth and gums; and feeling for fluid build up or bumps under the skin. Some simple tests are performed, such as a fecal examination to detect internal parasites or blood tests to detect contagious diseases. Thanks to these exams, your veterinarian will find most potential problems early enough to treat them. You

A healthy cat is a happy cat. Make sure that your Birman gets her annual veterinary checkup and that she eats properly and exercises.

All pet owners want a healthy and well-adjusted cat. Prevent illnesses and look out for any sudden behavior changes in your Birman, such as not eating or drinking more water than usual.

Relaxation is a big part of a cat's life, but if your Birman suddenly begins taking unusually long naps, take her to the vet for a checkup.

can aid in the effort throughout the year by performing home health exams and closely observing your Birman's condition and behavior to detect problems early and, if necessary, seek medical attention.

RECOGNIZING AN ILL CAT

Cats are adept at concealing illness and hiding discomfort they may feel to anyone but the most astute observer, so learning the danger signs of disease will go a long way in helping protect your cat. Being able to describe a symptom will help your veterinarian diagnose the problem. Different illnesses may have similar symptoms, so the more detail you can provide your veterinarian the better chance for a positive outcome.

Illness may reveal itself in both subtle or not so subtle behavioral changes that may or may not preclude overt physical signs that a health problem exists. Cats occasionally turn their noses up at the food their owners offer them, but if your cat seems disinterested in her meals altogether, it could signal a problem. If she does not eat for more than a day or exhibits other symptoms as well, contact your veterinarian. If your Birman is drinking more than usual or sitting with her head hanging over the water dish, it could be a sign or dehydration due to a fever, ingestion of a toxin, or to kidney problems.

Changes in litter box habits, such as urinating or defecating out of the box, are often thought to be behavior problems, but they may signal that something is physically wrong. It could be lower urinary tract disease or intestinal blockage. If your Birman suddenly exhibits an aversion to the litter box, have her examined by your veterinarian first before putting the cat on a behavior modification program.

If your quiet, gentle Birman turns suddenly aggressive or antisocial for no apparent reason, something physical may be wrong. Other behavioral changes that may mean your cat doesn't feel well include sleeping more than usual, hiding, crying for no apparent reason, listlessness, and loss of interest in her playthings and people.

Physical signs of illness may include vomiting or diarrhea. Cats often will vomit up a hairball or food if it does not sit well in their digestive systems. Likewise, they may occasionally have loose bowels. However, if the vomiting is repeated or the diarrhea lasts for more than a day, or if you notice blood in your Birman's stools or urine, see your veterinarian.

Cats that lose their desire to wash and exhibit a dull, lifeless coat may be showing the first signs that something is wrong. If your cat is constantly licking herself or washing so much that bald patches appear on her skin, it could indicate external parasites or allergies. Other overt physical signs of illness include

If your kitten hasn't already received the standard vaccination shots from the breeder, have the vet administer them.

wheezing, gagging or retching, sneezing, tearing or watery discharge from the eyes or nose, limping, hair loss or weight loss, seizures or fits, and lumps or bumps on or under the skin.

VACCINATIONS

As part of an annual checkup, your veterinarian will vaccinate your Birman against the more common feline diseases. Vaccines will force your cat's immune system to generate specialized proteins, called antibodies, that will help her develop resistance to bacteria, viruses, or toxins and fight off disease. By being exposed to the particular disease antigens, your Birman's immune system will fight off offending contagions.

Because your cat's immunity can decrease over time, she must be revaccinated, usually annually, at the time of her veterinary checkup.

If your Birman kitten has not been vaccinated already by the breeder from whom you obtained her, your veterinarian will administer a three-way series of shots called FVRCP. The shots typically are given in a series of two to three shots at three-week intervals, starting at the age of six to eight weeks. FVRCP vaccines help your cat fight off feline viral rhinotracheitis (FVR) and feline calicivirus (FCV), two of the more common and contagious respiratory diseases that infect cats. Both FVR and FCV account

Keeping your Birman inside will prevent her from contracting contagious diseases, like rabies. This pretty cat looks perfectly content hanging out in her basket.

Take special precautions when it comes to your Birman's health and have her checked regularly by a veterinarian.

If you have more than one cat, be aware of the feline leukemia virus, which can be easily transmitted through shared litter boxes and food and water bowls.

for the majority of feline respiratory diseases. Symptoms may include sneezing, coughing, and discharge from the nose and eyes. A cat with upper respiratory disease can become dehydrated and lose her appetite. Respiratory viruses live outside the body of an animal for several hours to several days and can be transmitted from one cat to another through direct contact or contact with contaminated cages, food and water dishes, bedding, and even the litter box of a diseased cat.

The third component of the vaccine will help your cat's immune system fight feline panleukopenia (FP), or as it's more commonly called, feline distemper—a highly contagious viral disease characterized by fever, loss of appetite, dehydration, vomiting, and a decrease in white blood cells.

Like the previous viruses, feline panleukopenia virus can be transmitted through direct contact with an infected cat and through contact with food bowls, litter pans, or bedding (also through contact with fleas during the acute stage of the disease). Kittens, because of their underdeveloped immune systems, are at greatest risk of contracting feline panleukopenia.

Rabies is caused by a virus that attacks the central nervous system of warm-blooded animals, and it can be transmitted from one species of animal to another. Your Birman cat can get rabies from the bite of a rabid animal or through infected saliva entering the body through an open wound, the eyes, or mouth. The end result of rabies infection is death.

Keeping your Birman indoors will go a long way toward preventing her from contracting rabies as well as other contagious diseases. Vaccinations will provide an extra measure of protection. Depending on where you live, you may be required by law to have your cat vaccinated against rabies and to schedule

Do everything you can to prevent your cat from getting fleas, which can live up to two years in your furniture or carpet.

booster shots every one to three years.

OTHER CONTAGIOUS DISEASES

If you obtained your Birman kitten or cat from a reputable breeder, she should be free of contagious diseases at the time of purchase. Reputable breeders routinely test their cats for contagious diseases. This prevents the cats from accidentally spreading diseases to other cats in their catteries and also prevents breeding stock from transmitting diseases to their offspring.

Feline leukemia virus (FLV) impairs a cat's immune system and makes the animal more susceptible to other illnesses, as well as decreasing her ability to fight off the effects of the disease. FLV is transmitted primarily via saliva and respiratory secretions, urine, and feces. Social grooming and licking, as well as sharing litter boxes and food and water bowls all make the leukemia virus easily transmitted from one cat to another in a multicat household. Cats roaming outdoors risk exposure from bite wounds from infected cats. A queen can transmit the feline leukemia virus to her offspring while they are in the uterus or while nursing via her milk.

Symptoms of FLV are often nonspecific. Poor coat appearance, loss of appetite and subsequent weight loss, lethargy, and stunted growth are some of the more common ones. Nearly one-third of cats exposed to feline leukemia virus develop a natural immunity to the disease and never become ill. Others may become latent carriers that either never succumb to the disease or show symptoms under stress or the onset of other diseases. The remaining FLV-positive cats die from the effects of the virus, usually within three years.

A test is available to detect FLV. If your Birman tests positive, have her retested within three to four weeks. If the resulting tests are negative, discuss FLV vaccination options with your veterinarian.

Feline infectious peritonitis (FIP) is a contagious and deadly disease that, like feline leukemia, has no cure. Laboratory tests can detect the presence of antibodies to combat coronaviruses, of which FIP is one. However, the test cannot specifically identify the FIP virus. Cats with the wet type of FIP will look extremely bloated in the abdominal area. If the fluid buildup occurs in the chest cavity, respiratory problems may occur. Other signs of FIP can include fever, loss of appetite, weight loss, and depression.

Even in catteries and multicat households, FIP is fairly uncommon. Most cats that contract FIP also have other immune-suppressing conditions, such as feline leukemia. There is a vaccine available to prevent FIP, but it has aroused much controversy since its introduction. If you keep your cat indoors and

If your cat develops a tapeworm, she will be robbed of her nutrition and develop a weakened immune system.

away from other cats with an unknown health status, you greatly lessen her chances of contracting FIP.

Feline immunodeficiency virus

Keeping your cat indoors can help prevent fleas. However, many products are available that can help remove fleas from floors, bedding, carpet, and furniture.

(FIV), commonly referred to as "feline AIDS," is another immune-suppressing virus for which there is no cure. Although the virus is similar to immune-suppressing viruses in other species, (including HIV, which affects humans,) it cannot be passed from cat to person and vice versa.

Transmission of FIV is thought to be through bite wounds from infected cats. Symptoms of FIV are difficult to pinpoint because a host of secondary infections such as anemia and low white blood cell count can occur. Mouth and teeth problems such as gingivitis, stomatitis, and periodontis are often the first signs of feline immunodeficiency virus.

An antibody test will confirm the presence of the feline immunodeficiency virus, but there is no vaccine available to prevent the disease. Keeping your cat indoors and away from infected cats is the best preventive measure you can take.

PARASITES

Parasites are organisms that obtain their food by living on or in a host animal, very often at the expense of the host's health and well-being. The more common external parasites that afflict cats include fleas, mites, and ticks. Among them, the most common and frustrating are fleas. If they make a home with you and your Birman, you may find them the most difficult to expel. Not only must you eliminate the adult fleas, but also the eggs and larva, which can live up to two years in your furniture and carpet.

If your Birman has become infested with fleas, you will notice flea dirt—bits of flea feces, ingested blood, and eggs—accumulating wherever your cat may sit or sleep. Even an indoor cat can get fleas, which can be carried in from the yard on your clothing and other pets. Fleas lay more eggs during warmer, more humid months, making them especially devastating during the summer or in warmer climates.

Fleas are not only painful and annoying to cats, they can also cause an allergic reaction, resulting in excessive licking and biting as well as subsequent hair loss. Keeping your Birman indoors will reduce the risk of her catching fleas, but it is no guarantee. Flea preventatives in pill form, such as Program™, have come on the market in recent years. When given regularly, they damage the flea eggs, thus breaking the flea life cycle.

There is a wide variety of products available, including sprays, powders, dips, shampoos, soaps, and disposable dampened topical cloths that can all help rid your Birman of fleas. Be sure to follow package directions and never mix products or use flea products intended for dogs on your cat. Foggers, misters, or premises sprays will help remove fleas from floors, bedding, carpet, and furniture.

Ear mites, which appear as a brown, cakey substance in a cat's ears, are microscopic parasites that can make your Birman shake her head, scratch her ears, or become restless. Although ear

Play is a natural thing for active kittens, but be sure to monitor their play closely to prevent unnecessary accidents from happening.

mites are annoying to your cat, they can be treated relatively easily and eliminated with medication.

If your cat has fleas or decides to have an infected mouse for her dinner, chances are she will develop a tapeworm—an internal parasite that can grow up to two feet in length in your cat's body. You most likely won't notice tapeworms until tiny segments resembling rice or sesame seeds are expelled. Your veterinarian will be able to treat the tapeworms, but you must rid your cat and your house of the fleas to prevent them from recurring. Tapeworms, like all parasites, can rob your cat of her nutrition or result in a weakened immune system if they are not eliminated from your cat's body.

Other internal parasites include roundworms, hookworms, and heartworms. To detect internal parasites, your veterinarian will conduct a fecal exam as part of your cat's annual checkup. He or she will then prescribe appropriate medicine to get rid of them.

SPAYING AND NEUTERING

One of the kindest things you can do for your Birman and yourself is to have female spayed or male neutered. The only reason to ever let your cat remain unaltered is as a participant in a legitimate breeding program associated with one of the pedigreed cat registries. To breed your cat simply to generate income, to allow a female to experience producing a litter, or to allow your children to experience the miracle of birth does a disservice to you, your cat, and cats everywhere.

Neutering a tom is a relatively simple procedure. Although performed under anesthetic, neutering is usually done on an outpatient basis, and the cat is allowed to return home the same day as the surgery. Leaving your male intact will promote a host of behaviors that are unpleasant for the owner as well as anyone visiting the home. Unneutered males mark territory by spraying an anal gland secretion that produces an offensive odor that is difficult to remove or mask. Once the odor is in your home, it will perpetuate itself by arousing your male to continue to mark objects around the house. He will spray not only when he detects the presence of an unspayed female, but also when he detects the presence of any other cat from which he wants to protect his territory. Once a male begins to spray, the habit is more difficult to break. Neutering will help prevent this behavior from ever occurring.

Spaying is a procedure in which the uterus of a queen is removed. Although it is more complex than neutering, spaying is a common procedure and should not be feared. The female usually remains in the veterinary hospital for one to three days following surgery and returns about ten days later for removal of stitches.

Just as male cats, unaltered females engage in behavior that causes owners some difficulty. An intact female when she enters estrus—the period of time when she is receptive to a male for the purposes of reproduction—will engage in behavior that is sexually suggestive to the male cat and annoying to her human companions. Rolling, crying, walking around with her posterior in the air, urinating more often, and dribbling watery discharge throughout her environment are some of the behaviors owners of unspayed females must endure.

Spaying is a common procedure and should not be feared. An unspayed female can engage in annoying behavior, such as rolling, crying, and urinating outside the litter box.

Veterinarians are altering cats at earlier ages, and the procedure should be performed no later than six to eight months of age. Discuss with your veterinarian the appropriate time to neuter or spay your cat.

FELINE FIRST AID

Keeping your cat indoors and catproofing your home will prevent a lot of accidents from ever happening, but sometimes even the best laid plans of mice and men can result in the unexpected. Cats don't always land on their feet, so falling or slipping can be a problem even inside the home. Ingesting a household chemical, chewing on an electrical wire, getting caught in a miniblind cord, burning feet on a hot surface or even getting too close to a candle flame are incidents that hopefully will never occur. However, being prepared might help save your cat's life in case one of them does.

If your Birman suffers an accident, a knowledge of first aid will help you deal with the situation. Keep your cool. Don't wait until an emergency happens to hunt for appropriate phone numbers or to determine how you should deal with the situation. Acting quickly and appropriately may help save your cat's life. Keep your veterinarian's phone number and the number of an off-hours emergency clinic near your telephone with other emergency numbers in case you need them. Purchase a book on first aid techniques and put together a first aid kit. Keep both handy.

BIRMAN HEALTH ISSUES

Breeders attest to Birmans being hardy cats with no health problems associated specifically with the breed. Some breed lines have been reputed to have problems with cardiomyopathy—a defect of the heart muscle that can ultimately cause heart failure—but it is unknown whether this condition is any more prevalent in Birmans than the cat population at large.

Birmans are a very hardy breed with no history of any major health problems.

EXHIBITING BIRMANS

As the owner of an Birman, eventually you will find yourself drawn to the world of the cat fancy, whether as an active participant exhibiting your cat in shows, or as a spectator. Even if your Birman is a pet-quality cat rather than a show-quality one, you are eligible to exhibit her in a cat show and compete with other pet-quality cats.

Cat shows are where breeders, cat owners, and cat product vendors can literally show off their wares. For the spectator, cat shows provide many opportunities to learn about cats, new cat-related products, and what constitutes a superb specimen of the breed.

ASSOCIATIONS AND CLUBS

There are more than half a dozen pedigreed cat associations in the United States and Canada, and additional ones exist worldwide that promote the cat fancy through regularly held shows. Even registries based in the US can boast international membership and shows held on foreign soil.

Record keeping is a primary function of the registries, which maintain the pedigrees of the cats and kittens of its members and guarantee that future offspring can be registered and ancestors can be traced.

Some registries allow individual memberships, while others offer membership through regional or

Even if your Birman is a pet-quality cat, you can still enter her in a cat show and compete with other cats of the same quality.

local cat clubs affiliated with the national association. The national and regional clubs as well as the registries are non-profit organizations whose goals center around promoting the cat fancy, the improvement of the individual breeds they recognize, and the welfare of cats in general. The Cat Fanciers Association, for example, supports the Robert H. Winn Foundation, a non-profit corporation that awards grants to research feline health-related studies and sponsors an annual symposium on current feline veterinary topics. Pedigreed cat registries take an active part in the community, encouraging spay/ neuter awareness, and their members become active volunteers at local animal shelters.

Registries have breed councils or committees, which serve as advisory bodies to the national associations. The Birman breed organizations are comprised of people who are knowledgeable and experienced with the breed, and

Cat shows are a great place to meet potential breeders and learn more about the breed of your choice.

who are responsible for the continued development of Birmans and for obtaining approval to modify to the breed standard.

SHOWS

Cat shows are the heart of the cat fancy. Breeding cats that conform to the standard of the breed is something to which all breeders aspire, and the cat show

These beautiful Birman kittens have the look of winners.

Cats compete against the breed standard rather than against one another. They are judged in separate, independently judged rings.

Cat shows are held worldwide and are governed by the rules and regulations of the sanctioning registry. Even US- based associations sanction shows in foreign countries and international shows within the US. An international show is quite an event. It can attract as many as 1,000 exhibitors from all over the world and as many as 10,000 visitors a day.

JUDGING

At a show, cats are judged in separate, independently judged rings. Cats compete against the breed standard rather than against one another. Each judging ring is presided over by a judge who is trained and licensed by the association in either specific breeds

provides the opportunity for them not only to exhibit the fruits of their labor but also to compete with their peers for awards and prizes.

The first cat show, which led to the birth of the cat fancy, took place in London's Crystal Palace in 1871. It wasn't until 1895 that a show held in New York City's Madison Square Garden marked the birth of the cat fancy in the United States.

Cat shows may be one,- two,- or several-day events, depending on the size of the sponsoring club. Shows can be classified as an all-breed show, in which all breeds and types of cats compete for awards, or a specialty show, in which only cats of a particular type or coat length compete.

Unlike an adult cat, a kitten does not have to be registered in order to compete in a show. "Indy" is most definitely the prettiest kitten in her class.

and categories or all breeds and categories. Depending on the registry, categories may bear the following names:

Championship: unaltered, pedigreed cats eight months of age or older.

Premiership: spayed or neutered cats eight months of age or older.

Kitten: pedigreed kittens aged four to eight months.

Provisional or NBC (New Breed or Color): for breeds that have not yet achieved championship status.

AOV (Any Other Variety): registered cats that do not conform to breed standards.

Household Pet: mixed breed or non-pedigreed cats.

To the untrained eye, competition can seem complex and confusing. By the time a cat is entered in a show, she will already have been determined to conform to a large degree to the acceptable standard of the breed, and it will be the judge's job to determine which among many beautiful specimens comes closest.

Once a cat has collected six first-place ribbons, she becomes a Champion. This Birman shows off her playing skills.

Before entering a show, it is wise to visit several as a spectator and watch the judging. Talk to exhibitors and familiarize yourself with the breed standards and categories in which you want to enter your Birman.

REGISTERING

It is common practice in the cat registries to allow an unregistered kitten to compete in a show. To be eligible to compete, adult cats must be registered. By The International Cat Association (TICA) rules, an unregistered adult can enter a show one time before being required to be registered with the association. The breeder from whom you purchased your kitten will have registered the litter when the kittens were born. The registry will return certificates for the individual kittens to the breeder to be passed along to the buyer. The buyer returns the certificate with the appropriate fees to the registry with the cat's chosen name to complete the process. If you have purchased an adult cat from a breeder, he or she should give you the registration certification at the time of purchase.

AWARDS AND PRIZES

Each registry awards predefined types of ribbons for the various categories of awards. Once a cat has collected six first-place ribbons, she becomes a Champion, after which she is eligible to compete against other Champions to garner points for Grand and Supreme Grand Champion status. Prizes awarded include ribbons, trophies, and/or cash.

Cats can register and compete in more than one registry, but points and awards do not carry over from one registry to another. A competing cat would have to start at the beginning and compete under the rules of each different registry.

ENTERING A SHOW

Cat shows are held virtually year-round, and the dates, locations, and entry fees are advertised in the major cat publications, as well as on the World Wide Web home pages of the cat registries. Before entering, obtain a copy of the show rules that describe entry procedures, eligibility, and exhibitor responsibility. After you have studied them, contact the entry clerk to request a show flyer and entry form. Send the completed form and fees by the deadline specified. You will receive confirmation by mail.

As one progresses from local to national and international shows, the competition becomes steeper. The exhibition Birman must be a exemplary example of her breed and her coat must be in beautiful condition. She must be alert and playful, yet passive enough to be handled by the judge. Competing cats must be healthy, and in some cases, are required to have a veterinary inspection prior to the show. Your Birman must be free of contagious diseases. She must be well-behaved and able to withstand the stress and rigors of the show hall environment. Stressful conditions include being caged for most of the day, being

Whether your Birman is a champion show cat or a pet, she is still a beloved and cherished companion.

handled by judges whom your cat does not know, and tolerating the constant peering eyes of show spectators. Prior to the show, cats must be bathed and groomed and their nails clipped.

AT THE SHOW HALL

Once at the show, your Birman will be assigned a number and a cage in what is called the benching area, where cats wait to be called into the judging ring. Shows typically represent a lot of commotion, but as an exhibitor you must pay attention to what is being announced over the public address system so that you don't miss being called.

Cages are typically decorated and carry the cattery name if the cats inside are being shown by a breeder. They also may display ribbons already won by their occupants. In addition to any decorations you may desire, you will need a carrier for your cat, a litter box, a cat bed or blankets, food and water dishes, a supply of your cat's food and water, grooming tools, a first aid kit, paper towels, vaccination certificates, and a show catalog. The show committee will provide cat litter. If you decide to enter your cat in a show or simply attend as a spectator, make the experience an enjoyable one.

HOW TO CONTACT THE REGISTRIES

Following are the major pedigreed cat registries in the US and Canada.

American Association of Cat Enthusiasts, Inc. (AACE)
Box 213
Pine Brook, IL 07058
913-335-6717
info@aaceinc.org
http://www.aaceinc.org

American Cat Association (ACA)
81901 Katherine Avenue
Panaorama City, CA 91402
818-781-5656

American Cat Fanciers Association (ACFA)
P.O. Box 203
Point Lookout, MO 65726
417-334-5430
info@acfacat.com
http://www.acfacat.com/

Canadian Cat Association (CCA)
220 Advance Blvd., Suite 101
Brampton, Ontario, Canada
L6T 4J5

Cat Fanciers' Association (CFA)
Box 1005
Manasquan, NJ 08736
cfa@cfainc.org
http://www.cfainc.org/

Cat Fanciers' Federation (CFF)
Box 661
Gratis, OH 45330
513-787-9009
http://www.cffinc.org/

The International Cat Association, Inc. (TICA)
Box 2684
Harlingen, TX 78551
210-428-8046
http://www.tica.org/

INDEX

Adam, Madame Marcelle, 7
Adult cats, 11, 21, 22
Africa, 41
American Kennel Club (AKC), 15
Angora, 6
Association of American Feed Control Officials
     (AAFCO), 39
Awards, 62
—Championship, 20
AOV, 61
Backyard breeder, 27
Bathing, 36, 37
Birmanie, 3
Burma, 3
Burmese, 3
Cardiomyopathy, 57
Cat Fanciers Association (CFA), 7
Cat Fanciers Association, Inc., 15
Champion, 62
Color, 19, 20
—blue point, 20
—chocolate point, 20
—lilac point, 20
—seal point, 20
—white blaze, 25
—white gloving, 25
Crystal Palace, 60
Declaw, 32
Diseases, 52-55
Ear mites, 54
Exhibiting, 58
Feeding, 39-45
Feline calicivirus (FCV), 49
Feline distemper, 51
Feline immunodeficiency virus (FIV), 53, 54
Feline infectious peritonitis (FIP), 53
Feline leukemia virus (FLV), 52, 53
Feline panleukopenia (FP), 51
Feline viral rhinotracheitis (FVR), 49
First aid, 57
Fleas, 54
Food, 43
—dry, 43
—semi-moist, 43
—wet, 43
French cat fancy, 7
FVRCP, 49
Gingivitis, 54
Gordon, Major Russell, 6
Grand Lama, 4

Grooming, 31-38
—tools, 36
Hairballs, 35
Health, 30
Heartworm, 55
Himalayans, 7
Hookworm, 55
Household pet, 61
Illness, 47
Kittah, 4
Kittens, 11, 21, 22, 61
Lao-Tsun, 3
Lower Urinary Tract Disease (LUTD), 45, 48
Madison Square Garden, 60
Maldenpour, 6
Mites, 54
Multicat environments, 9, 52, 53
Mun Ha, 4
National Birman Fanciers, 7
Neutering, 30, 55
Parasites, 54
Pavie, August, 6
Periodontis, 64
Persians, 7
Pet quality, 15, 24, 26
Premiership, 61
Provisional, 61
Rabies, 51
Robert H. Winn Foundation, 59
Roundworm, 55
Sacre de Birmanie, 7
Sacred Cat of Burma Fanciers, 7
Safety, 34
Scratching, 32
Show quality, 15, 25, 26
Siamese, 6, 11
Sinh, 4
Sita, 6
Spaying, 30, 55
Stomatitis, 54
Stud service, 23
Tapeworm, 55
The International Cat Association (TICA), 61
Ticks, 54
Tipping, 25
Toxicity, 42
Toys, 13, 33
Tsun-Kyan-Kse, 4
Vaccinations, 49, 51
World War II, 7

INDEX

Adam, Madame Marcelle, 7
Adult cats, 11, 21, 22
Africa, 41
American Kennel Club (AKC), 15
Angora, 6
Association of American Feed Control Officials
    (AAFCO), 39
Awards, 62
—Championship, 20
AOV, 61
Backyard breeder, 27
Bathing, 36, 37
Birmanie, 3
Burma, 3
Burmese, 3
Cardiomyopathy, 57
Cat Fanciers Association (CFA), 7
Cat Fanciers Association, Inc., 15
Champion, 62
Color, 19, 20
—blue point, 20
—chocolate point, 20
—lilac point, 20
—seal point, 20
—white blaze, 25
—white gloving, 25
Crystal Palace, 60
Declaw, 32
Diseases, 52-55
Ear mites, 54
Exhibiting, 58
Feeding, 39-45
Feline calicivirus (FCV), 49
Feline distemper, 51
Feline immunodeficiency virus (FIV), 53, 54
Feline infectious peritonitis (FIP), 53
Feline leukemia virus (FLV), 52, 53
Feline panleukopenia (FP), 51
Feline viral rhinotracheitis (FVR), 49
First aid, 57
Fleas, 54
Food, 43
—dry, 43
—semi-moist, 43
—wet, 43
French cat fancy, 7
FVRCP, 49
Gingivitis, 54
Gordon, Major Russell, 6
Grand Lama, 4

Grooming, 31-38
—tools, 36
Hairballs, 35
Health, 30
Heartworm, 55
Himalayans, 7
Hookworm, 55
Household pet, 61
Illness, 47
Kittah, 4
Kittens, 11, 21, 22, 61
Lao-Tsun, 3
Lower Urinary Tract Disease (LUTD), 45, 48
Madison Square Garden, 60
Maldenpour, 6
Mites, 54
Multicat environments, 9, 52, 53
Mun Ha, 4
National Birman Fanciers, 7
Neutering, 30, 55
Parasites, 54
Pavie, August, 6
Periodontis, 64
Persians, 7
Pet quality, 15, 24, 26
Premiership, 61
Provisional, 61
Rabies, 51
Robert H. Winn Foundation, 59
Roundworm, 55
Sacre de Birmanie, 7
Sacred Cat of Burma Fanciers, 7
Safety, 34
Scratching, 32
Show quality, 15, 25, 26
Siamese, 6, 11
Sinh, 4
Sita, 6
Spaying, 30, 55
Stomatitis, 54
Stud service, 23
Tapeworm, 55
The International Cat Association (TICA), 61
Ticks, 54
Tipping, 25
Toxicity, 42
Toys, 13, 33
Tsun-Kyan-Kse, 4
Vaccinations, 49, 51
World War II, 7